TH
WHI

~ BOOK ~

Judy Ridgway

GUILD PUBLISHING
LONDON · NEW YORK · SYDNEY · TORONTO

© 1989 Judy Piatkus (Publishers) Limited

This edition published 1989 by
Guild Publishing by arrangement with
Judy Piatkus (Publishers) Ltd

CN 2417

Drawings by Trevor Newton
Cover photograph by Theo Bergström

Printed and bound in Great Britain

CONTENTS

The vine after woodcut
by Petrus De Crescentiis
from 'Liber Ruralium
Commodorium' first
published in 1471

INTRODUCTION

'Wine is the alcoholic beverage obtained from the fermentation of the juice of freshly gathered grapes, the fermentation taking place in the district of origin according to local tradition and practice.'

This is the EEC definition of wine and it includes all the essential elements which go into making wine. 'Wines' from fruit other than grapes are not included in the definition.

Surprisingly, the exact nature of fermentation was not fully understood until about a century ago and wine-making could be a very chancey business. Modern technology has meant that much of the guesswork has been taken out of cultivating vines and making wine, but fine wines still depend on considerable care and skill from both grower and maker.

HISTORY OF WHITE WINE

Wine-making originated in ancient Persia. Vines were cultivated on the southern slopes of the Caucasus Mountains flanked by the Caspian and the Black Sea. From Persia the craft spread in all directions, but the Babylonians became particularly keen wine-makers. There is even a wine list dating from the time of King Nebuchadnezzar in existence today.

Wine-making skills spread to the shores of the Mediterranean. Soon the Greeks and the Romans had the vine and both rated the commodity it produced so highly that they each dedicated a god to wine. The Greek Dionysus and the Roman Bacchus were both high-ranking deities.

The Romans carried the vine inland. They developed frost-proof vines and planted them in Bordeaux and along the Rhône, Marne, Seine,

Mosel and Rhine valleys. Vines even found their way as far east as Hungary and as far west and north as York, England.

The Romans were converted to Christianity and as their empire collapsed and the legions returned to Italy and the East, the early Christian missionaries and monks carried on the skills of viticulture and wine-making. They needed sacramental wines and so wherever they built a church, they planted a vineyard.

The Dark Ages saw little progress in wine production. Some wine came to England via the Netherlands, and in Spain the Moors – rather surprisingly in view of their Muslim faith – improved the culture of the vine there.

The Norman conquest of England coincided with an upsurge in demand for wine all across Europe. The marriage of Eleanor of Aquitaine to King Henry II of England opened the way for the Bordeaux wine/English wool trade. Wines from Gascony, Poitou, Burgundy and Languedoc were also shipped in vast quantities, some finding their way into other parts of Northern Europe. The wines certainly reached Scotland, where Alexander III managed to run up a bill of £2,000 – no mean sum in those days – to one Gascony merchant!

The French wars in the fourteenth century meant friendship between England and Spain, and this in turn encouraged Spanish wine imports to the UK. This trade continued into the sixteenth century when sack (similar to present-day sherry) became the favourite wine. Sack also provided the German word for sparkling wine – Sekt. In the nineteenth century Ludwig Devrient, an actor, became famous for his playing of Falstaff. After the theatre and still in character he would call for 'a cup of sack' at the local wine cellars. He actually meant a glass of champagne or a sparkling wine, and so Sack or Sekt became synonomous with sparkling wine in Germany.

Wines from Germany continued to flow west to the Netherlands and England, and in Georgian times the Hanoverian connection swelled this trade. German wine was often known as Rhenish, but Hockheimer was often referred to as Hockamore. This gives a much earlier origin to the word hock which is often attributed to Queen Victoria's love for the wine.

The twentieth century has seen a number of changes in the pattern of the wine trade. Exports of port to the UK, once the major outlet for this drink, started to fall and by the late Twenties sherry had become a more popular wine for social drinking. However, this too has now lost its major position and table wines have taken over as one of the most popular drinks.

The last twenty years have seen the emergence of a major challenge to Europe's traditional wine-producing areas in the development of a flourishing wine-making business, first in California and, more recently, in Australia and New Zealand. Regions which do not grow their own wine now have a much greater choice on the off-licence or supermarket shelf than ever before.

GRAPES AND GRAPE VARIETIES

Wine is made from a specific type of grape called *Vitis vinifera*. These grapes are used only for making wine. They are not table grapes and would probably taste very bitter if you tried to eat them.

Grapes are made up of a thick skin which contains colour and a central pulp which has little or no colour at all. The skins can be removed from red grape varieties and the resultant wine will be white, or nearly white. The so-called blush wines are often made in this way from red grapes such as Cabernet Sauvignon. Red Pinot Noir grapes are used without skins in the manufacture of champagne.

As well as colour, the skins also contain tannin which is bitter and usually not wanted in white wine. The pulp contains sugar, fruit acids, water and pectins, all of which are important in wine-making.

On the outside of the grapes is a whitish bloom. This waxy substance traps three organisms which are important in wine-making. These are wild yeasts, wine yeasts and bacteria. The wild yeasts and bacteria are not wanted in the wine-making process, but they need air to live and so can be eliminated by being deprived of it. The wine yeasts which are wanted, are able to work in the absence of oxygen.

There are many different varieties of *Vitis vinifera*. Originally, each grape variety grew in one particular part of Europe. However, some grape varieties, such as Chardonnay and Sauvignon Blanc, were considered to produce a better wine than some of the others and so their use spread to other parts of Europe and more recently to the New World.

The best grape varieties for producing fine wine are known as 'classic grapes'.

CLASSIC GRAPES

CHARDONNAY: This is probably the most sought after single grape variety in the world today. It grows well in countries as far afield as California, Australia and Bulgaria, as well as in Spain, Italy and France. In fact, there is hardly a significant wine-producing country which is not experimenting with Chardonnay.

Burgundy is the area originally associated with Chardonnay and here the grape produces long-lasting wines with a very elegant, almost honied or buttery flavour. In the New World, the wine made from Chardonnay becomes almost more full-bodied and opulent, and 'tropical fruits' is a favourite phrase used by wine experts to describe the flavour.

Very often, Chardonnay wines are aged in oak casks and the combination of flavours is quite distinctive. Wood ageing of Chardonnay began in Burgundy, but is now also carried out in Australia and in California.

RIESLING: This is the great grape variety of Germany and it is sometimes known as the Rhine Riesling. It is grown in many countries around the world, but it always retains its own distinctive character. The wine produced from the grapes varies from very dry to extremely sweet, but it always has a wonderful flowery smell and taste, which matures to a spicy oiliness.

When the conditions are right (see page 13), the Riesling grape is attacked by 'noble rot' and some very complex wines can result. The best wines, with or without 'noble rot', age very well and can be kept for ten or twelve years without any deterioration.

SAUVIGNON BLANC: This grape has been grown for centuries in the Loire and Bordeaux regions of France, but it is only in this century that it has come to be appreciated as a great wine-maker. Sauvignon wines are dry and refreshingly zesty with a characteristic grapefruity or gooseberry flavour to them.

In France, this grape is used to make Pouilly Fumé, Sancerre and Bordeaux Blanc, in the latter sometimes blended with Semillon. Elsewhere, it is used to make varietal wines, some of which are oak-aged and often called Fumé Blanc, or Blanc Fumé. Australia and California both have good examples. New Zealand is the newest of the wine-making areas to produce really good wines from the Sauvignon grape, but experiments are also going on in Spain, Portugal and Italy.

SEMILLON: In its original home of Bordeaux, and in one or two other places such as Australia's Hunter Valley, this grape can produce stunning wines with great ageing capacity. This is the grape which, with Sauvignon Blanc, produces the great Sauternes, but it is also used to make drier wines in both Bordeaux and other areas of the world.

Semillon is particularly susceptible to noble rot and when this does attack the wines produced will usually be outstanding.

The biggest plantings of Semillon outside France are in Chile, where it is responsible for about three quarters of all the wine produced. In Australia Semillon is blended with other varieties such as Chardonnay and Trebbiano.

CHENIN BLANC: This is probably the least appreciated of the white classic grapes for it can indeed produce very indifferent wines. But, at its best, it produces extremely long-lasting sweet wines of great character. It is used in the Loire to make Vouvray and Coteaux du Layon.

NON-CLASSIC GRAPES

ALIGOTE: The second white grape of the Burgundy area.

GEWÜRZTRAMINER: A German grape with a very distinctive aroma and taste. It is almost spicy and can taste of lychees. It is also grown in Alsace and in Italy, North America and New Zealand.

MÜLLER THURGAU: A cross between Riesling and Sylvaner. It is one of the varieties grown in the UK.

MUSCAT: The grape which produces wine with a distinctly grapey flavour. It is usually used in the production of sweet wine, but in Alsace it is used to make a completely dry wine.

PINOT GRIS: Closely related to Pinot Blanc. These grapes are grown in Alsace and in Northern Italy.

SYLVANER: A declining grape variety originally grown in Germany. Other newer varieties are taking over from it.

TREBBIANO: The grape used in a large quantity of Italian wine.

GROWING VINES

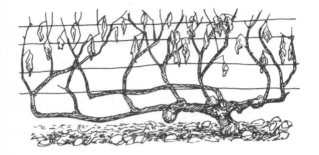

Vines need plenty of sunshine in summer to ripen the grapes. They also need a cool enough winter to enable them to rest and gather strength for the coming growing season. In the northern hemisphere the northern limit is set around latitude 50° and the southern limit at 30°. In the southern hemisphere the latitudes are reversed. Within these 'wine' belts vines will grow well but some varieties will tolerate the lack of sun or excess heat at the edges rather better than others.

In England, for example, there is only sufficient sun to fully ripen a grape crop in the open in two years out of five, and it is not possible to guarantee a frost-free period when the flowers are forming. This means that English growers can really only grow white grape varieties, which generally need less sun to ripen them than red ones.

The soil, too, plays an important part, but there is a saying that the best wines come from the poorest soils. The vine seems to flourish where other crops will not. The vine does not need nitrogen as much as other plants, but what it does need is plenty of mineral elements in the soil. These are essential to the delicate flavours of different wines. Volcanic soils, limestone, chalk and granite all produce different styles of wine.

The microclimate and the soil of a small area or even a single vineyard can affect the qualities of the finished wine to such an extent that an expert wine taster will be able to identify exactly where the grape was grown.

GRAFTING

Nowadays most vines are grated on to American root stocks. This is to protect them from a root-eating plant louse which almost completely destroyed European vineyards in the late nineteenth century. The louse, Phylloxera, came to Europe from America, and the American vines were found to be resistant. The only problem was that these American grapes gave a very distinctive 'foxy' taste to wine which was not much liked. The answer which the farmers finally came up with was to graft European vines on to American root stocks and, except in a few isolated places, that is the way vines are now grown throughout the world.

THE VINEYARD YEAR

In the northern hemisphere the vineyard year starts after the vintage in late October or early November when the vineyards are generally tidied. The land is ploughed and soil is built up around the roots to protect the vine during the winter. December and January see the continuation of general maintenance.

February is the main pruning season and cuttings are taken from grafts. Pruning is finished in March, the roots are cleared of soil and grafting starts. In April the shoots begin to grow and are fastened to the wires or trellises in the vineyards. This is followed by the first spraying in May and flowering and pollination in June. Planting of new sections of the vineyard takes place in May.

Spraying will continue as necessary through the summer and in July the grapes will be clearly visible. There may be a summer pruning now to allow more light and sunshine to reach the fruit and to stop the leaves from taking over. The grapes begin to swell and change colour in August and the wine-making equipment is prepared. In September the grapes are nearing maturity and they are tested for sugar. The harvest generally runs from mid-September to mid-October.

NOBLE ROT

When the weather conditions are right *Botrytis cinerea* or noble rot attacks the ripe grapes. This usually happens when the autumn is hot, but not humid. The conditions have to be exactly right or the noble rot turns to grey rot and the harvest is ruined.

Botrytis cinerea is a fungus which looks quite disgusting. It is grey and dusty, but its effect is to raise the sugar content of the grape and to increase the acidity. It also adds a wonderful raisiny caramel flavour to wine made from the shrivelled grapes.

Semillon and Riesling are the grapes most likely to be affected by noble rot and the results can be tasted in top-class Sauternes and in German and Austrian Trockenbeerenauslese wines.

Wine comes in at the mouth
And love comes in at the eye;
That's all we shall know for truth
Before we grow old and die.

A Drinking Song
William Butler Yeats (1865–1939)

HOW WHITE WINE IS MADE

Wine-making depends on the action of yeast enzymes converting the sugar from the grapes into alcohol. The process is known as fermentation. Gas and heat are given off as well as alcohol, and the whole mixture bubbles and ferments.

At the winery the grapes are crushed and the wine yeasts on the skins and the sugar in the pulp come together. The skins are not needed for colour or tannin, so are immediately removed. A few wine-makers do leave white wine on its skins for a few days and this can give it a more interesting flavour.

The next step is to add sulphur to the grape juice, or 'must'. This kills off any wild yeasts and bacteria by excluding air. Sometimes the must is also cleared at this time.

Fermentation starts almost immediately and the temperatures reached can be very high indeed. Cooling is essential to produce a good white wine and in many areas special equipment has been installed to ensure a cool fermentation.

The fermentation is allowed to continue until the sugars present have been used up and a completely dry wine results, or it may be stopped in order to retain residual sugar. This is done by centrifuging the yeasts out of the wine, filtering them or killing them by fortifying the wine with alcohol.

After fermentation the wine is allowed to rest for a few weeks and then is drawn, or racked, off its lees (the sediment of yeast and pulp). Some wines, such as Muscadet, may be left to mature on their lees.

Most white wines are racked and bottled during the year following the harvest. However, a few – usually wines which have a high acidity level, such as Burgundy, or which are very sweet, such as Sauternes – are matured for longer. This may be in oak casks, which impart a distinctive flavour.

White wines are very susceptible to spoilage when they come into contact with oxygen and so sulphur dioxide is used to protect the wine throughout its various stages.

ROSÉ WINES

Apart from some pink champagnes, rosé wines are not made by blending red and white grapes or the resultant wines. Instead, they are made either by fermenting the must of red grapes for a very short time on their skins, or by using the free-run juice from very well-coloured red grapes which is sufficiently tinted to be identified as rosé.

FORTIFIED WINES

Fortified wines such as sherry, Madeira and Marsala have a higher percentage of alcohol than light or table wines; alcohol is added during production.

Major White Wine Producing Regions

America

California is the most important wine-growing area in the United States of America. The same grape varieties are grown here as in Europe. They include Chardonnay and Chenin Blanc, together with some Sauvignon, Semillon and Riesling.

The vines are planted in the valley floors and on the lower slopes. The Nappa Valley was one of the first areas to produce fine wines and many of the best known wineries are there.

Most of the wines are produced as varietal wines from one grape variety rather than from blends. If a variety is stated on the label, the wine must contain at least 75% of that variety. The best wines tend to be fairly full-flavoured.

Oregon and Washington States are both making great strides in producing wines comparable to those of California. Chardonnay is the most successful white variety.

AUSTRALIA

White wine production is relatively new in Australia and most of them are produced as varietal or single grape wines. These must contain a minimum of 80% of the named variety. The predominant grape varieties are Rhine Riesling, Chardonnay, Chenin Blanc and Semillon. The latter is also known as Hunter Riesling.

The wines are very fruity and full-flavoured with a distinctive taste of their own. Many people describe the flavours as 'tropical fruits'. The best ones can hold their own with any of the great French wines. Some of the best-known areas are the Hunter Valley and Murrumbidgee Irrigation Area in New South Wales, Rutherglen in Victoria, the Barossa Valley in South Australia and the Swan Valley and Margaret River areas of Western Australia.

AUSTRIA

White wine is the mainstay of the Austrian wine business and much of it is based on a local grape, the Grüner Veltliner. Riesling is also grown quite widely and used for dessert wines rather similar to, but stronger than, those made in Germany.

BULGARIA

The state-run wine industry in Bulgaria has developed some very good value-for-money white wines which find their way mainly to the West. They are based on the Chardonnay grape which is grown in eastern parts of the country, particularly at Shumen. Some Sauvignon and Riesling is also being tried out. Some of the wines are aged in oak casks and these are generally more interesting than the others.

CHILE

The vineyards of Chile are remarkable in that they have never been attacked by the root louse phylloxera and so all the vines grow on their own root stocks.

The original vineyards were developed by the Spaniards and some of the best vines today are made by Spanish companies. The main grape varieties are Chardonnay, Semillon, Sauvignon and Riesling. Some of the wines are aged in wood for quite long periods of time and they take on a very oaky flavour which can be a bit of an acquired taste.

ENGLAND

After a slow start, England now produces quite a respectable quantity of wine. Most of the grape varieties grown are German varieties and most of the wine is similar in style, though maybe slightly drier than German wine.

It is important to distinguish English wine from British wine. English wines are table wines of the EEC made from fresh grapes grown in the UK. British wines are made from dried grapes or concentrated juice and they come under the category not of tables wines, but 'made wines'.

FRANCE

BORDEAUX is probably best known for its red wine, but it does also produce quite large quantities of straightforward white Bordeaux AC. This may be made from Sauvignon or Semillon grapes alone or from a blend of the two. The best white wines from Bordeaux come from Sauternes and Barsac. These are sweet wines, which have been attacked by noble rot and aged in oak casks. There is a classification system for the best chateaux. Chateau d'Yquem is the most famous of them all. Unfortunately, a certain amount of very boring Sauternes is also produced. This is sweet and sticky and has no character at all. Price is the main guideline. The handpicking and sorting required for grapes which have been attacked with noble rot is very high and the wine is fairly rare.

BURGUNDY is the great dry-white-wine producing area of France. The best wines are made from the Chardonnay grape and in a good year have great ageing potential. Lesser wines are sometimes made from the Aligote grape.

The finest wines are made in the regions of the Côte de Nuits at Chambolle-Musigny and in the Côte de Beaune at Corton Charlemagne, Puligny-Montrachet and Meursault. Further south, there are the first-class Pouilly Fuissé wines along with Montagny, Rully and Mâcon.

LOIRE is a very important white-wine-producing area and grapes are grown almost continuously along its banks from Nantes in the west to Sancerre in the east.

Muscadet production is centred on the Nantes region and this wine has been growing in popularity year by year. Luckily, there is plenty of designated land where the grape can be grown.

As you continue up river, the principal grape variety grown changes to Chenin Blanc, but Sauvignon is also grown in small quantities in Touraine and Haut Poitou. Wines are generally medium dry or sweet if made from Chenin Blanc and dry if made from Sauvignon. Sancerre and Pouilly-sur-Loire even further up river are the great Sauvignon-producing areas. The wines are very fine and can last for two or three years.

This area is also well-known for its rosé wines. Anjou Rosé is probably the best known.

RHÔNE VALLEY is predominantly a red-wine area, but some dry white wines are also produced from local grape varieties. The best are Condrieu and Hermitage.

ALSACE, in northeastern France, is another of the major white-wine-producing areas of France, though unlike Burgundy and the Loire it is far less well-known outside France. It also differs from the other areas in that most of the wines are only produced as varietal wines. These include Pinot Blanc, Riesling Tokay, Gewürztraminer and Muscat.

All the wines are very fruity, but they are also almost all dry. A very few sweeter wines are produced from late-picked grapes in particularly good years.

GERMANY

Germany is the great white-wine-producing country of Europe. It lies at the limit of the northern climatic band wherein grapes can be grown for wine, and red varieties do not flourish.

The classic grape of Germany is the Riesling and in the right circumstances it produces beautifully mellow and long-lasting wines. Other grape varieties include Müller-Thurgau and Sylvaner, but the percentages of the latter are declining.

Most of the vines grow on the steep-sided valleys of the Rhine and its tributaries and grapes are left to ripen until the last possible moment. Because the wines produced can be very acidic, the practice of adding unfermented grape must, or susswein, has grown up and this results in medium-dry to medium-sweet wines.

The finest wines are called Qualitätswein mit Prädikat (QmP) wines and by law may not have any sugar added to them at all. German wines are classified not only by the area in which the grapes are grown, but also by the sugar content of the grape must. The best wines are, in increasing order of sweetness, Kabinett, Spätlese, Auslese, Beerenauslese and Trockenbeerenauslese.

Probably the most famous of all Germany wines is Liebfraumilch, which is a Qualitätswein bestimmte Anbaugebiet (QbA) wine, or a wine from a designated quality region. This is the grade immediately below QmP. Liebfraumilch gets its name from wine which used to be made from grapes in the vineyard of the Church of Our Lady, the Liebfrauenkirche in Worms, and the name has stuck to branded wines from four of the German wine regions.

Wines from the Rheingau are considered to be among the very best that Germany can produce. They are closely followed by wines from the Nahe and the Moselle.

Liebfrauenkirche
Worms

GREECE

The best-known Greek wine is Retsina. This is a white wine which has been resinated. It is made quite simply by the addition of resin to the wine during production. The resin was originally added to form a film over the wine and so prevent oxidation, but with long exposure the Greeks have come to acquire a taste for wine flavoured with strongly scented resins. Kokkineli is the rosé version.

HUNGARY

White wines are produced in some quantity around the shores of Lake Balaton and in the central plain of Hungary. They are mainly based on the Eastern European grape varieties.

The northeastern part of the country produces the distinctive Tokay wines from the Furmint grape. Aszu berries – carefully selected grapes which have been affected by noble rot – are crushed by their own weight in tubs called puttonyi. Their juice is collected and the aszu berries are pounded into a paste and added to the normal wine. The proportions in which the aszu berries are added determine the final quality and sweetness. The fermented wine is left to mature for six or seven years in unbunged casks. The end result is an extremely long-lasting wine with great depth and complexity.

ITALY

Today, northern Italy produces some very drinkable white wines. The problems of making white wine in a hot climate have been largely overcome by the use of cold fermentation techniques. The growers, too, have been experimenting with new methods and with growing new varieties of grapes.

Trebbiano is the most widely grown traditional grape, but in the northeast Riesling, Chardonnay and Gewürztraminer are popular. The popular Soave is produced around Lake Garda and this is made from Trebbiano mixed with Garganega.

Further south, Trebbiano again turns up, this time in Orvieto. Other grapes and wines include Vernaccia de San Gimignano from Tuscany and Verdicchio from the Marche.

NEW ZEALAND

This is an area which is eminently suited to the production of white wine and in recent years the New Zealanders have been producing some very good wines indeed.

Müller-Thurgau is the most widely planted grape variety, but it is the Sauvignon Blanc which is currently attracting most attention outside of New Zealand. Chardonnay, too, is coming rapidly to the fore and some of these wines are aged in oak.

The wines are less aggressive than Australian wines and some of them can easily be mistaken for European wines.

PORTUGAL

The best-known white wine from Portugal is Vinho Verde which comes from Minho in the northwest of the country. The name Vinho Verde doesn't really mean that the wine is green in colour, but rather refers to the youth of the wine and to the surprisingly green countryside in which the grapes are grown.

The grapes are harvested in October and then fermented, cooled, filtered and bottled ready to drink in February. The wine has a slight prickle to it and is best drunk as young as possible.

SOUTH AFRICA

The vineyards in South Africa were first planted in 1652 and some of the old estates, such as Constantia, are still producing wine.

The most common varieties are Riesling – both Cape Riesling and the more recently planted Rhine Riesling – Colombard, Semillon, Chenin Blanc (also known as Steen) and Palomino, which is used to make South African sherry.

SPAIN

Rioja is probably the best wine-producing area of Spain. The white wines vary in character though they are all made from local grape varieties. In the past, the Spaniards always aged their white wines in oak casks alongside their reds. This produced a very distinctive flavour which was not so popular outside of Spain. So, when Spain entered the EEC and started to export larger amounts of wine, they changed the way in which they made their white Rioja. Today, most of the white wine from the region is fresh and crisp with no oak ageing at all.

Penedès wine-producers, in contrast to those of Rioja, are experimenting with non-Spanish grape varieties such as Chardonnay and Sauvignon Blanc. Some of the wines are made from a simple variety, but others are made from a blend using new and traditional grapes such as the Parallada.

YUGOSLAVIA

White wines in Yugoslavia are made from Eastern European grape varieties such as the Olaz riesling. Lutomer Riesling is probably the best-known wine from this area.

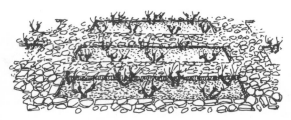

CHAMPAGNE

Wines with a sparkle mean a celebration and champagne is the acknowledged leader in the field. The secret of making champagne was discovered by accident some 300 years ago, when it was noticed that in warm weather some wines tended to ferment again in the bottle and become effervescent. Dom Pérignon, who was the abbot at the abbey of Hautvillers, is often connected with the discovery. Whether that is true or not is debated by Spanish sparkling-wine-makers in Penedes, but he certainly had the idea of using reinforced stoppers to hold the wine in.

HOW CHAMPAGNE IS MADE

The modern *méthode champenoise* is quite a long and complicated process. Grapes are bought in by the champagne houses after the harvest, but the wine-makers will have been monitoring all that went on in the vineyard during the preceeding year.

The grapes are gently pressed and only the first two thirds of the juice of each pressing goes into the best champagnes. The must is fermented slowly and the resulting wines are blended to produce a consistent flavour. After blending, small amounts of sugar syrup and yeast are added. The wine is then bottled in strong bottles and placed in deep, cool cellars for at least a year and often more than three years.

During the second fermentation in the bottle a deposit is formed. This is eventually removed by gradually upending the bottles in special racks, slowly turning them and increasing the angle fractionally every day for several weeks. The deposit slides down to the cork where it is eventually frozen and ejected. The small quantity of lost wine is made up with a dosage of champagne and syrup. The amount of this added liquor determines the final degree of sweetness.

CHAMPAGNE CONSUMPTION

Champagne is exported all over the world, but the UK takes more than other countries, including the USA. The figures for 1988 are as follows:

Country	No. of bottles
UK	20,648,000
USA	14,508,000
West Germany	12,307,000
Switzerland	8,565,000
Italy	8,435,000
Belgium	5,478,000
Netherlands	1,594,000
Australia	1,374,000
Canada	1,068,000
Spain	893,000

CHAMPAGNE BOTTLES

Large bottles are increasingly popular today. Here are the accepted sizes for champagne bottles.

Magnum	— contains 2 bottles
Double Magnum	— contains 4 bottles
Jeroboam	— contains 4 bottles
Rehoboam	— contains 6 bottles
Methuselah	— contains 8 bottles
Salmanazah	— contains 12 bottles
Balthazar	— contains 16 bottles
Nebuchadnezzar	— contains 20 bottles

At the other end of the scale there are also half and quarter bottles.

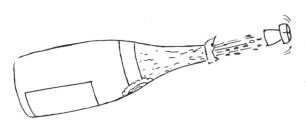

There is a tavern in the town,
And there my dear love sits him down
And drinks his wine 'mid laughter free
And never, never thinks of me.

Song (Anon.)

29

SPARKLING WINES

There is a whole host of sparkling wines from countries as likely as France and as unlikely as India, made in the same way or in a different way from champagne. At present, those which are made in the same way as champagne may be labelled '*méthode champenoise*'. From 1993, this will be forbidden outside the champagne region.

Sparkling wine is also made by the *cuve close* or *charmat* method in which the second fermentation takes place in closed tanks instead of in the bottles. Such wines are less expensive to produce. A few rather inferior sparkling wines are quite simply carbonated.

Here is a roundup of some of the world's sparkling wines.

France
Loire: Saumur; Vouvray
Burgundy: Cremant de Bourgogne
Alsace: Cremant d'Alsace
South of France: Clariette de Die;
Blanquette de Limoux

Spain
Penedès: Cava (*méthode champenoise* only)

Germany

Sekt and Deutsche Sekt (the latter is only
    made from grapes grown in Germany;
    the former is made in Germany, but
    the grapes may be grown anywhere in
    the EEC)

Italy

Piedmont: Asti Spumante

Sparkling wine is also made in Bulgaria, Australia,
California, England, Hungary, New Zealand, South
Africa and India.

CHOOSING SPARKLING WINES

The terms used to show the dryness or sweetness of
champagne and sparkling wine, in order from the
driest to the sweetest, are Brut or very dry, Extra Sec
or extra dry, Sec or dry, Semi-Sec or medium-dry
and Doux or sweet.

If the bottle or neck label indicates a year, it is
'vintage' champagne or sparkling wine, made only
from the grapes of that year. For champagne and
some sparkling wines, if no year is shown it is a
blend from different years, made by the producers
to a house style.

SERVING WHITE WINE

WINE AND FOOD

White wines are usually served with starters and fish courses. A really full-bodied white wine might accompany poultry, and sherry is traditional with soup. These generalisations can be quite useful, but there is no need to follow them slavishly.

What is important is to choose a wine which is both to your taste and complementary to the food. There is no reason why you should not drink white wine with the meat course or, indeed, with the cheese, if you wish. And champagne, that wonderful wine, will partner even foods such as asparagus, caviar and smoked salmon which are normally considered difficult to match.

Muscadet and Chablis are crisp and dry wines which seem to go particularly well with shellfish and white fish. Other suggestions might be a New Zealand or Californian Sauvignon or a Sancerre. Oily, more strongly flavoured fish go well with the fuller-bodied Chardonnay or Semillon wines from Australia.

The only way to find out what goes best with what is to experiment. After all, some classic meat dishes are cooked in white wine and well-flavoured wines, such as Alsace Gewürztraminer, Californian Blanc Fumé and Spanish white Rioja, will partner even the most robust of meat dishes.

Sweet white wines or dessert wines are usually

served with the pudding, but they can also be served earlier in the meal, perhaps with very rich or strongly flavoured pâtés. They also go well with blue cheese.

Oriental food can be difficult to accompany, but Mateus Rosé seems to have taken over the Indian and Chinese restaurant wine list. Vinho Verde can also be very good with these types of food.

TEMPERATURE

The traditional advice was to serve white wine at cellar temperature. This may have been useful when most wine drinkers had a cellar! Today, the advice is to serve white wine chilled. However, this is not really all that much more helpful as the domestic refrigerator, set at around 9°C or lower, can soon make the wine too cold.

Ideally, sherry and Madeira should be served at 10°C, champagne and most dry white wines at about 9°C, and sweet whites wines at between 5 and 6°C.

For most wines an hour in the fridge will be quite sufficient, but the very best method for chilling wine quickly is to place the bottle in a bucket of water, with a couple of trays of ice cubes. This is much more efficient than ice cubes alone.

OPENING WINE

A good corkscrew is the only really essential piece of equipment needed by a wine lover. Remove the capsule which covers the top of the bottle as this is made of lead, then draw the cork and wipe the mouth of the bottle with a clean cloth to remove any mould or dirt.

Champagne corks are under pressure and should be treated with some care. Make sure that the cork is not pointing at anybody when you remove the wiring. Gently ease out the cork, using your wrist to prevent it from bursting out too fast. Use champagne pliers if the cork is very tight.

Very occasionally wine is 'corked'. This does not refer to the fact that some of the cork may have crumbled into the wine, but means that the cork has been contaminated with a mould which gives off a very nasty smell.

White wines do not usually throw a sediment and so do not need to be decanted. However, yellowish-white tartaric crystals do sometimes form. This is usually due to a change of temperature and indicates that the wine has not been centrifuged to death. These crystals are not harmful. Simply pour the wine carefully, leaving the crystals in the bottom of the bottle.

GLASSES

A good glass should have a stem long enough to give a comfortable grip and a foot wide enough to give a steady base. Do not fill the glass too full as space should be left to enjoy the bouquet. Tulip-shaped glasses and Paris goblets are fine for serving most kinds of white wine.

Sparkling wine should be served in slightly taller or fluted glasses to charm the bubbles up in long, attractive trails. Old-fashioned saucer-shaped champagne glasses dissipate the bubbles, are easy to spill and have no space for the aroma.

A man may surely be allowed to take a glass of Wine by his own fireside.

Memoirs of the Life of The Rt. Hon. Richard Brinsley Sheridan (1751–1876)

WHITE WINE COCKTAILS AND CUPS

KIR

This is a twentieth-century drink devised by a famous French priest, named Canon Kir. The Canon became a senior member of the French National Assembly and was for years Mayor of Dijon. He died in 1968 aged 92 and his favourite tipple has increased in popularity ever since.

The original recipe is as follows:

Per glass:

1 teaspoon crème de cassis
chilled Bourgogne Aligote

Place the crème de cassis in the base of a glass and top up with the white Burgundy.

Variations:
* Any kind of dry white wine can be used, but it must be dry.
* Blackcurrant syrup can be substituted for crème de cassis, but it will not have quite the oomph of the real thing. Ribena will *not* do!

KIR ROYALE: Here a sparkling white wine is used with the crème de cassis instead of a still wine. Try a sparkling Crémant de Bourgogne or a sparkling Saumur from the Loire.

PEACH ROYALE: A similar wine and liqueur idea has swept across the fashionable world recently. This uses a peach liqueur in place of crème de cassis.

CHAMPAGNE COCKTAIL

Every barman worth his salt has his own version of this. These are the basic ingredients per serving:

1 cube sugar
a dash Angostura bitters
1–2 teaspoons brandy
iced champagne

Place the sugar cube in the base of a champagne flute and add the Angostura bitters and brandy. The brandy should just cover the sugar cube – any more and the champagne will be drowned. Top with iced champagne.

Variations:
* Replace one teaspoon of brandy with Grand Marnier
* Replace all the brandy with Eau de Vie de Framboise

BUCK'S FIZZ

The French call this drink Mimosa. It is made with equal quantities of champagne and orange juice. It should be made with freshly squeezed orange juice, not the concentrated orange juice out of a carton.

BLACK VELVET

This very British drink is made with half champagne and half stout or Guinness.

BARBARA WEST

1 measure gin
1 measure sweet sherry
1/2 measure lemon juice
dash Angostura bitters

Stir with ice and strain into cocktail glasses.

GUNGA DIN

2 measures gin
1/2 measure dry vermouth
1 measure orange juice

Shake with ice and strain into cocktail glasses.

DUBONNY

1 measure gin
1 measure Dubonnet
$1/2$ measure dry sherry
$1/2$ measure dry vermouth

Stir with ice and strain into cocktail glasses.

NEW YORKER

1 measure gin
1 measure dry vermouth
$1/2$ measure dry sherry
1 teaspoon Cointreau

Stir with ice and strain into cocktail glasses.

HAVANA

1 measure white rum
1 measure cream sherry
$1/2$ teaspoon lemon juice

Shake with ice and strain into cocktail glasses.

Measure = 1 fl oz (25 ml)

WHITE WINE ZIP

This is a refreshing cocktail to serve on a hot day. It is not too alcoholic, but has lots of fruity flavour. German wine is very good for this recipe.

4 fl oz (100 ml) medium dry white wine
1 tablespoon lemon juice
2 ice cubes
1 teaspoon orange squash

Pour the wine into a glass and stir in the lemon juice, with the ice cubes. Top with the orange squash and serve at once.

Serves 1

SPRITZER

The practice of watering wine with a little water probably started at the German spa towns where the various spa waters were sometimes served with a little wine. Today, a mixture of white wine and a sparkling water, such as soda, Perrier or Buxton, makes a refreshingly low-alcohol drink. Use half and half dry or medium white wine and sparkling water. Add a slice of lemon or lime for a change.

WHITE WINE PUNCH

Punch gained its name from India, where travelling Britons quenched their thirst in long, cold mixes containing local produce. For no apparent reason, it became the custom to use just five ingredients: spirits, tea, fruit juice, sugar and water were the most usual. The Hindi word for five is *pantsch* and this easily became punch when spoken by the British.

Here's a good version for serving before a barbecue or at a summer garden party.

2 pints (1.2 litres) medium dry white wine
1/2 bottle dry sherry
1 miniature bottle brandy
4 fl oz (100 ml) lemon juice
1/2 pint (300 ml) strong cold tea
soda water
ice cubes
cucumber slices

Mix together the first five ingredients and chill well. Just before serving, add a siphon of soda water and serve in glasses with ice and cucumber.

Serves 18

Who does not love wine, women and song
Remains a fool his whole life long.

Attrib. Martin Luther (1483–1546)

SUMMER STRAWBERRY CUP

The strawberry flavour of this cup is greatly
enhanced if you use a bottle of strawberry-flavoured
German wine from the House of Hallgarten.

8 oz (225 g) fresh strawberries, washed
2 tablespoons sugar
juice of 1 lemon
4 fl oz (100 ml) brandy
1 bottle sweet white wine, chilled
1 bottle light red wine, such as Valpolicella
1 pint chilled soda water
ice cubes

Cut the strawberries into quarters or slice them.
Place them in a bowl with the sugar, lemon juice and
brandy and leave to stand until required. Stir in the
wines and soda water and serve with a few pieces of
strawberry and an ice cube in each glass.

Serves 18

SPARKLING FRUIT CUP

Serve this sparkling fruit cup on a special occasion.
Start with the full quantity of sparkling wine
(Spanish Cava is a good choice) and make refills with
two bottles of wine and one of lemonade. (If you
cannot find maraschino or grenadine syrup, a few
sugar cubes should sweeten the cup sufficiently.)

3 bottles chilled sparkling dry white wine
5 fl oz (125 ml) brandy
3 fl oz (75 ml) Cointreau
3 fl oz (75 ml) maraschino or grenadine syrup
ice cubes

Mix all the ingredients in a large bowl or jug as near as possible to the time you are to serving the cup. Do not stir too much or you will lose all the bubbles. Serve in flutes with a small lump of ice in each.

Serves 18–20

SHERRY AND MOSCATO PUNCH

This mixture needs to be very well chilled, so mix at least two hours in advance.

1 bottle medium dry sherry
¼ bottle brandy
1 miniature bottle Cointreau
2 tablespoons grenadine syrup
1 bottle chilled Asti Spumante
1 chilled siphon soda water

Mix the sherry, brandy, cointreau and grenadine syrup in a large jug or bowl and chill well. Add all the other ingredients and serve at once.

Serves 18

DRY TO SWEET WINE GUIDE

A guide to the sweetness of white wines has been drawn up by the Wine Development Board in London. It uses a simple nine-point scale identified by the numbers 1 to 9.

The guide is intended to help new wine drinkers to find their way around the most important part of the taste characteristic of white wine – the sweetness. It will also help those who would like to experiment with wines they have never tried before.

The guide is a voluntary one, but many supermarkets and off-licence chains use the symbols on their wine shelves. The EEC Commission has made amendments to the relevant regulations for still white wines to enable member countries to use the guide on their labels if they so wish.

Starting at 1, the wines are bone dry and may be quite sharp and fresh. At 9, at the other end of the scale, are the really sweet wines, such as Muscat de Beaumes-de-Venise and Madeira.

1

Bergerac	Chablis	Sancerre
Muscadet	Entre-Deux-Mers	Champagne
Touraine	Pouilly Blanc	Manzanilla sherry
Saumur	Fumé	Tavel rosé

2

Graves
Riesling d'Alsace
Frascati Secco
Orvieto Secco
Verdicchio
Soave
Chardonnay

Méthode Cham-
    penoise, Cava
    and Sekt
Dry Vouvray
Trocken German
    wines
White Rioja

White Burgundy
White Rhône
Spanish dry white
Fino Sherry
Dry sherry types
Dry Montilla
Sercial Madeira

3

Pinot Blanc
    d'Alsace
Brut sparkling wine
Muscat d'Alsace
Halb-Trocken
    German wine
Hungarian Olasz
    Riesling dry

Grüner Veltliner
    Austria
Gewürztraminer
    d'Alsace
Dry Amontillado
    sherry
Medium dry
    Montilla

Medium dry
    vermouth
Dry white
    vermouth
Dry white port
Anjou Rosé

4

Vinho Verde
Chenin Blancs
Moselle Kabinett
Other Gewürz-
    traminer
Rhine QbA
EEC wines
Moselle Deutscher
    Tafelwein

Moselle QbA
Rhine and Nahe
    Kabinett
Yugoslave Laski
    and Hungarian
    Olasz
Riesling medium
    dry
Australian, New

Zealand and
    Bulgarian Rie-
    slings
Full Amontillados
Medium dry
    sherry types
Portuguese rosé
Orvieto Abbocato

5

Rhine Deutscher
    Tafelwein
Moselle Spatlesen
Vouvray Demi-Sec

Austrian Spätlesen
Liebfraumilch
Rhine Spätlesen
Medium British

sherry
Verdelho Madeira
Medium white port

6

Demi-Sec sparkling and Demi-Sec champagne	Tokay Szamarodni sweet Spanish medium	All golden sherry types

7

Asti Spumante Moselle Auslesen Rhine Auslesen Tokay Aszu Premières Cotes de	Bordeaux Monbazillac Pale cream sherry Montilla cream Bual Madeira	Rosso, rosé and bianco Vermouths

8

Moselle Beerenauslesen Austrian Beerenauslesen Rhine Beerenauslesen	Moselle Trockenbeerenauslesen Spanish sweet wine Moscatels Sauternes Barsac	Dark cream sherry Cream and rich cream sherry types

9

Rhine and Austrian Trockenbeerenauslesen Eiswein	Malmsey Madeira Muscat de Beaumes-de-Venise	Marsala Brown sherry Moscatels

Here with a loaf of Bread beneath the bough
A flask of wine, a Book of Verse – and thou
Beside me singing in the Wilderness –
And Wilderness is Paradise enow.

The Rubayat of Omar Khayam
Edward Fitzgerald (1809–83)

STORING WHITE WINE

Most white table wines are designed for immediate drinking, but some do benefit from a while in store. This can vary from six months to a year for non-vintage champagne and lesser Burgundies to four to eight years for fine wines, such as Meursault and Puligny-Montrachet from Burgundy, top-class German wines and Sauternes. Others, Madeira and Chenin Blanc wines such as Coteaux de Layon, will benefit from even longer.

Having wine to hand in your home is also very convenient. It means that you will always have something to offer the unexpected guest and won't have to bring home carrier bags of wine very time you entertain.

Starting a cellar or stock of wine does not necessarily mean that you have to have a real cellar in the basement. Understairs cupboards, old refrigerators or freezers located in the garage or even racks in the kitchen can all be pressed into service.

The ideal cellar has a constant temperature, is dark but damp-free and has good ventilation and no vibration. However, the most critical factor is temperature. This should be between 10 and 15°C and, most importantly, there should be no sudden changes in the temperature.

The wine should be stored in racks so that the bottles are lying on their sides. This ensures that the cork is in contact with the wine. If the bottles are stored upright, the cork dries out and air gets into the bottle, spoiling the wine. The exceptions are Madeira and sherry, where the alcohol may attack the cork.

Do remember to keep some sort of list of the bottles you have in store and, if you are using more than one storage space, where each one is located. Failure to do this could well mean that you will keep a wine longer than is sensible and you may find that it has deteriorated.

VINTAGES

Unless the climate is constant, the quality of the wine produced in a region will vary from year to year. Set out opposite is a vintage chart for European wines, based on a scale of 0 to 7 (0 is poor and 7 is exceptional). These ratings give a general idea of the standard of wine produced in a given region in a given year, but individual wines may be much better or much worse than the average. For a detailed assessment you really need to know how the individual growers fare that year. Wines from outside Europe do not usually have such a big difference between vintages.

Years	Sauternes	Burgundy	Champagne (vintage)	Germany
1988	5	6	—	5
1987	5	4	—	4
1986	6	6	—	5
1985	5	6	6	6
1984	4	4	—	3
1983	6	6	5	5
1982	5	6	5	4
1981	5	5	6	5
1980	4	5	5	4
1979	5	7	6	3
1978	5	6	6	4
1977	4	5	—	3
1976	6	6	6	7
1975	6	5	7	6
1974	5	5	—	4
1973	5	6	6	5
1972	3	3	—	3
1971	5	6	6	7
1970	6	7	6	4

RECIPES

WINE SOUP

There are a number of versions of this soup from various Central European countries. This one comes from Austria.

3 egg yolks
1/4 pint (150 ml) Austrian dry white wine
1/4 pint (150 ml) double cream
1/2 pint (300 ml) chicken stock
pinch cinnamon

Beat the egg yolks with the wine and pour into the top of a double saucepan. Add the cream and stock. Cook over gently boiling water, stirring all the time until the mixture thickens. Serve in individual bowls, sprinkled with cinnamon.

Serve 4

MOULES MARINIÈRE

Make sure the mussels are thoroughly clean by placing them in a bucket of water sprinkled with oatmeal for 6–8 hours. Remove them from the water 10–15 minutes before using.

4 pints (2.5 litres) mussels, well scrubbed
6 shallots, finely chopped
2 sticks celery, finely chopped (optional)
1 oz (25 g) butter
pinch dried thyme or savory
1 bayleaf
½ pint (300 ml) dry white wine
2 tablespoons freshly chopped parsley

Fry the shallots and celery, if using, in the butter in a deep saucepan. Make sure all the mussels are tightly closed and add them to the pan. Toss over a medium heat and leave the lid on. After a short while (2–3 minutes) the mussels will open. Add the dried herb and wine and bring to the boil.

Simmer for a further 5 minutes. Serve sprinkled with freshly chopped parsley.

Serves 4

FONDUE

Swiss Fondue is usually made with a strong spirit such as kirsch or schnapps, but in France the choice is white wine. For a particularly interesting flavour, use a distinctive wine such as Alsace Gewürztraminer.

1 clove garlic
½ pint (300 ml) well-flavoured white wine
1¼ lb (550 g) Gruyère cheese, grated
3 oz (75 g) Brie or Camembert, diced
1 tablespoon cornflour
1 tablespoon brandy
cubes of crusty bread or lightly toasted white bread

Cut the clove of garlic in half and rub it around the inside of the fondue dish or pan. Add the wine and heat until bubbling. Add the cheese and stir over a gentle heat until it has all melted. Mix the cornflour and brandy and stir into the fondue. Cook for a further 1 to 2 minutes until the mixture thickens. Keep warm and serve with bread or toast cubes.

Serves 4–6

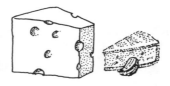

Coq Au Riesling

This dish is often on the menu of Alsatian brasseries in Paris and is also popular back home in Alsace. Here is quite a rich version which is suitable for any kind of entertaining.

4 chicken breast fillets, skinned
1 oz (25 g) butter
1 tablespoon cooking oil
16 baby onions
½ bottle Alsace Riesling
¼ pint (150 ml) double cream

Fry the chicken breasts in the butter and oil until lightly browned. Remove from the pan and fry the baby onions. Return the chicken to the pan with the wine. Bring to the boil, cover and simmer for 20 minutes.

Remove the chicken and onions from the pan and keep warm. Add the cream and boil rapidly to reduce the sauce. Pour over the chicken and serve.

Serves 4

Hillside in Alsace

SALTIMBOCCA

The Italians make this Roman dish with Marsala, Sicily's delicious fortified wine. However, you could use any kind of fortified white wine to hand.

350 g (12 oz) fillet of veal, thinly sliced
75 g (3 oz) Parma ham, thinly sliced
16 leaves fresh sage
75 g (3 oz) butter
150 ml (5 fl oz) Marsala or sweet sherry
2 slices white bread, crusts removed

Place the slices of veal between two pieces of greaseproof paper and flatten out by beating with a heavy object. Cut into 16 small pieces. On each one lay a sage leaf and a slice of ham. Roll up and secure with a cocktail stick.

Melt half the butter in a saucepan and cook the veal rolls until they are brown all over. Add the wine and bring to the boil. Boil for one minute and then reduce the heat. Cover and simmer for 10 minutes until the meat is cooked through.

Meanwhile, melt the remaining butter in another pan and fry the bread slices on each side until crisp and golden. Drain on kitchen paper and cut into triangles. Use to garnish the saltimbocca.

Serves 4

SYLLABUB

This dish started off life as a simple bowl of freshly drawn milk. The story has it that Charles II liked to watch his cows being milked in St. James's Park and then take a bowl of the frothy milk mixed with wine. Today whipped cream is used in place of milk to give a much thicker and richer dessert.

¼ pint (150 ml) white wine
strips of lemon rind, pith removed
3 oz (75 g) caster sugar
½ pint (300 ml) double cream

Pour the wine into a bowl and add the lemon rind. Leave to stand until required. Remove the lemon rind. Stir in the sugar and keep stirring until it has mostly dissolved. Add the cream and whisk until soft peaks form. Serve with little biscuits.

Variation:
This also makes a very good ice-cream, but because of the high fat content it should not be kept in the freezer for more than a week.

Serves 4–6

WINE VINEGAR

Vinegar is a medieval word which literally means sour wine. The wine is attacked by the acetobacter bacterium and this results in an acetous fermentation in which the alcohol in the wine is changed to acetic acid.

The first vinegar was probably made by accidentally leaving some wine out in the hot sun. Sherry vinegar is made in much the same way today. The sherry producers quite simply half-fill casks with Oloroso sherry and place them in the full heat of the sun. The wine then turns naturally to vinegar.

Other types of vinegar are made using wooden vats filled with small coils of wood which are impregnated with acetobacter. The wine is trickled in at the top and allowed to trickle through to the bottom. The wine gradually turns to vinegar and is drained off.

However, the most modern way of making vinegar is in an acetator. Here the wine is placed in a large vat with a starter culture of acetobacter. Warm air is passed through the wine to bring it up to 30°C. All the wine will be converted to vinegar in about fifteen days.

White wine vinegar can be made from any kind of white wine and from champagne and sherry. It is used as the base for all kinds of salad dressings, pickles, marinades and vinegar-flavoured sauces. Some white wine vinegars are flavoured with herbs or spices, such as tarragon, garlic, dill or nutmeg.

Wine And Medicine

Wine is the second oldest disinfectant in the world. The victim who fell among the thieves in the parable of the Good Samaritan had his wounds washed with wine. The acidity and alcoholic content of wine can be useful in the absence of TCP or other disinfectants.

Cleopatra is reputed to have thrown pearls into a cup of wine. When the pearls dissolved, she drank the resulting potion in the belief that it would prolong her youth.

Cures For Hangovers

Unfortunately for most of us, excessive consumption of wine leads to a hangover. There are probably as many cures for the condition as there are sufferers.

'Hair of the dog' is a common remedy which involves drinking a small amount of alcohol to counteract the excesses of the day before. Top of this list is ice-cold vintage champagne.

Perhaps more sensible cures include the use of vitamin C and the B complex vitamins. Alcohol tends to destroy these vitamins and so they will need to be replaced after drinking. Alcohol also causes the body to dehydrate and it makes sense to replace this water as soon as possible. Always try to drink at least as much water as you have drunk wine.

DREAMING OF WINE

Vines

* Dreaming of vines is one of the luckiest dream omens there is, but only if the vines are healthy and in leaf.

* If they are in blossom you will be successful beyond your wildest dreams.

* But it is bad news if the vines are withered or dry, for this means that you are overtaxing your strength and should slow down for a while.

Wine

* Dreaming of the wine itself is also a good omen. It can mean health, happiness and prosperity.

Corks

* Dreaming of pulling a cork signifies good news, and to hear the pop of a champagne cork indicates that a light-hearted love affair is just around the corner.

* To see a cork on its own means money luck.

ACKNOWLEDGEMENTS

The author and publisher would like to thank the following organisations for their help with information and statistics.

The Wine Development Board,
Five Kings House,
Kennet Wharf Lane,
Upper Thames Street,
London EC4V 3BH

Send a stamped self-addressed envelope for leaflets on Mulled Wines, Summer Wines and Sparkling Wines.

The Wine and Spirit Association
of Great Britain and Northern Ireland,
Five Kings House,
Kennet Wharf Lane,
Upper Thames Street,
London EC4V 3BH

OTHER TITLES IN THE SERIES

The Little Green Avocado Book
The Little Garlic Book
The Little Pepper Book
The Little Nut Book
The Little Mushroom Book
The Little Rice Book
The Little Tea Book
The Little Coffee Book
The Little Chocolate Book
The Little Curry Book
The Little Mediterranean Food Book
The Little Exotic Vegetable Book
The Little Exotic Fruit Book
The Little Yoghurt Book
The Little Tofu Book
The Little Breakfast Book
The Little Egg Book
The Little Potato Book
The Little Spice Book
The Little Herb Book
The Little Sherry Book
The Little Whisky Book
The Little Red Wine Book